LET'S EXPLORE
CORAL REEFS

SPEEDY
PUBLISHING

Speedy Publishing LLC
40 E. Main St. #1156
Newark, DE 19711
www.speedypublishing.com

Copyright 2015

Coral reefs are often called the "rainforests of the sea".

A coral reef is a community of living organisms. It is composed of plants, fishes, and many other sea creatures.

Coral reefs are the most diverse ecosystems in the world, housing about 25% of all marine life on the planet.

Coral reefs are built from stony corals, which in turn consist of tiny invertebrate animals called "polyps" that cluster in groups.

Each polyp is linked by a living tissue to form a community. The top layer of a coral reef contains living polyps.

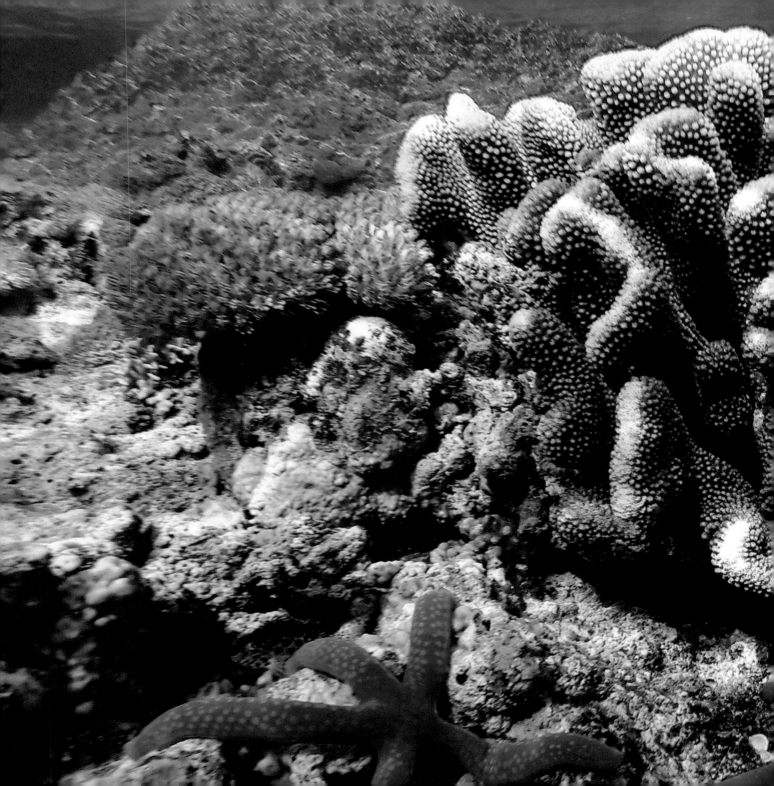

Corals excrete hard calcium carbonate exoskeletons which support and protect the coral polyps.

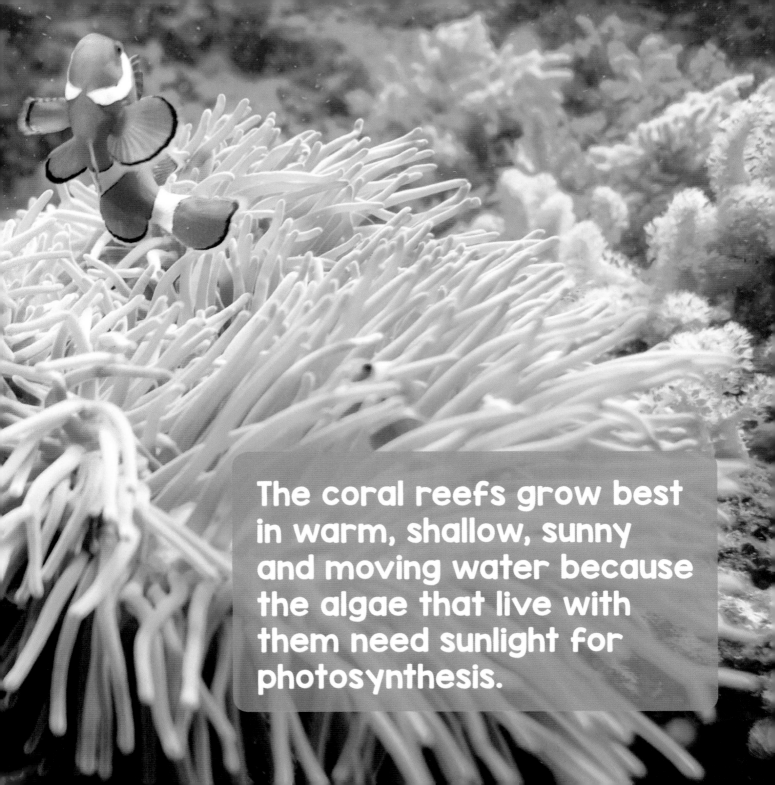

The coral reefs grow best in warm, shallow, sunny and moving water because the algae that live with them need sunlight for photosynthesis.

Coral reefs take a very long time to grow. They grow at a rate from 0.3 cm to 10 cm per year.

The coral reefs we see today have been growing over the past 5 000 to 10 000 years.

Coral reef are naturally colorful because of the algae. If the coral reef appears white, this means there is a pollution problem.

Although many types of animals live within the coral beef, it has much more diversity in its plant life.

Coral reefs are an important location for finding food, shelter, mates and places to reproduce.

The numerous types of seaweed, plankton and algae type growths that thrive on a coral reef provide food for an amazing amount of fish.

Reefs also act as nurseries for large fish species, keeping them safe until they are large enough to go into the deeper ocean.

Printed in Great Britain
by Amazon